Aubrey, Evan, and the Hurricane

Jennifer Bauer

NEWMAN SPRINGS PUBLISHING
320 Broad Street
Red Bank, NJ 07701

First originally published by Newman Springs Publishing 2018

ISBN 978-1-64096-132-6 (Paperback)
ISBN 978-1-64096-136-4 (Hardcover)
ISBN 978-1-64096-135-7 (Digital)

Printed in the United States of America

For Aubrey and Evan,
thank you for the inspiration.

And Mike, I'd weather any storm with you.
xoxo

Lauren, Matt, Owen & Leo - thank you
for keeping us safe and distracted during
Hurricane Irma. You turned our evacuation
into a vacation and I'm forever grateful.

Aubrey and Evan loved their new house. They had just moved in when their mom surprisingly said it was time for them to leave again.

"What? Where are we going?" asked Aubrey.

"We're going to evacuate," their mom said. "It means we're going to leave for a little while and take a road trip because there is a big storm coming. Pack some of your clothes and favorite toys then put them in the car. We're leaving in the morning."

Aubrey and Evan were sad. They didn't want to evacuate. They wanted to stay at their house and play with their friends.

As they packed the car and prepared to leave they saw their neighbor, Gabriela.

"What are you doing?" Gabriela asked.

"We are evacuating," said Evan. "Our mom says a storm is coming, something called a hurricane, and we need to get away from it before it arrives."

Gabriela knew all about hurricanes. She had been through them before.

"My mom and dad said we're going to stay here during the hurricane," Gabriela explained. "We have food and extra water and flashlights in case the electricity goes out."

8

Aubrey and Evan were jealous. They wanted to stay in their house, just like Gabriela.

"Some families stay and others evacuate during a hurricane," their mom said. "It's up to the grown-ups to decide what is best for each family. The most important thing is to stay safe and stay together."

11

The next day, as Aubrey and Evan drove away, they waved goodbye to Gabriela.

"Goodbye!" they shouted. "We'll see you after the storm passes. Be safe!"

For the next few days, Aubrey and Evan stayed with their cousins who lived far away. They were safe from the hurricane and had fun playing together but they worried about their friends back at home.

They saw on TV that a lot of rain was falling and the winds were very strong. Some of the tall, thick palm trees were even starting to bend. It was scary.

Once the hurricane was gone, it was time for Aubrey and Evan to return home. They made the drive back to their house but it took a long time.

As they got closer, they saw a lot of trees down and broken fences. Even their favorite playground was badly damaged.

"The wind did that," their dad explained. "Hurricanes have very powerful winds and bring lots of rain."

Part of the roof of their house was missing and some of their toys were broken.

"Oh no!" cried Evan. "I'm so sad. I really liked this basketball hoop and now it's ruined."

"All of this stuff can be repaired or replaced," said their mom. "The most important thing is we were together as a family and we're safe."

Just then, Gabriela came running outside. She was excited to see her friends.

"Welcome back!" she said. "I missed you."

Gabriela's house was also damaged during the hurricane. There were some broken windows, her favorite playhouse came apart in pieces and the pool in Gabriela's backyard was full of leaves and dirty debris.

"I was scared when the hurricane was here," admitted Gabriela. "It was dark, very windy, and there was a lot of rain. Some of the streets started to fill up with water. They were flooded."

27

Just like Aubrey and Evan's mom and dad, Gabriela's mom and dad made sure she was safe during the storm too.

Now the friends were together again and could start to clean up the mess left behind by the hurricane.

"Come on," said Aubrey. "I've got a broom. Let's get to work!"

About the Author

Jennifer Bauer is mom to the real-life Aubrey and Evan. She wrote this book for them after they evacuated their home because of Hurricane Irma in September, 2017. Bauer spent nearly two decades as a television news reporter covering hurricanes and other natural disasters around the country. She now resides in Parkland, Florida with her children and husband, Mike.

CPSIA information can be obtained
at www.ICGtesting.com
Printed in the USA
LVHW021944230520
656399LV00012B/225